For Pearl

HILLSIDES

Poems & Tales
Donald J. Heffernan

Lone Oak Press ◆ **Rochester, Minnesota**

Lone Oak Press
Box 9006
Rochester Minnesota 55903-9006

Some of the poems in *Hillsides* have previously appeared in: *Best Poets of 1988* (California), *VYNL Arts Magazine* (Minnesota), *American Poetry Anthology* (California), *The Northfield Magazine* (Minnesota), *Kings Review* (California), *Credenza* (Minnesota), *Castles in the Air* (Colorado), *World of Poetry* (California), *Parnussus* (Colorado), *AAUW* (Minnesota), *The Lamplight* (Nebraska), *Northern Sun* (Minnesota), *Pundit* (University of Missouri), *Paintbrush* (University of Missouri).

Copies and bulk-order information are available from:
Lone Oak Press
Box 9006
Rochester, Minnesota 55903-9006

ISBN   0-9627860-0-4
First Edition

Illustrations by Marilyn Taus on front and back covers and Pages x, 3, 5, 8, 52, 56, 75 and 78, and by Lee Capsadle on Page 30. Photograph of the author on Page 86 by James Crnkovich.

Thanks for graphic assistance by Dr. Todd Holmes and Cary Perket.

Hillsides was edited and designed by Ray Howe of Lone Oak Press and typeset and printed by Jack Miller and Pauline Redmond at their Anvil Press shop in Millville, Minnesota.

*Drawings by Marilyn Taus, appearing on the cover
and throughout* Hillsides, *convey a unique feeling.
Here is Marilyn on her work and on* Hillsides:

*"These are drawings from my private collection.
I call it my Heritage Portfolio. It is work done in
Northern Minnesota — a place of refuge and renewal
for me. My family is from Grand Marais — my
grandfather was a pioneer who built Clearwater Lodge
up the Gunflint Trail. I learned to see up there...
"I'm very happy to be part of Don's book —
poetry: another kind of soul food — an appropriate
place to show these drawings that represent a place
that can nurture one back to inner health when
depleted."*

*Marilyn Taus makes her living from her art. Her
paintings have been exclusively in oil for the past
five years.*

CONTENTS

1   Ancestors on Hillsides
4   Birch Lake
6   Kitchigumi
7   Another One for the Road Please
9   American Menu
10 Manual for Lovers
11 Hot Water
     (for Amos Owen, the Pipe Carrier)
15 Sirens
17 Corn Vows
18 Eighteen and Leaving
19 Twelve
21 Photoland
23 Chernobyl: A Clean Sweep
25 A Tribute to a Young Russian Painter
26 Mr. City On Sabbatical
29 An Autumn Hillside
31 Conversion
32 Escape From Tomorrow
33 Paper Airplanes
34 Just Another Apocalypse
40 A Hilly Perspective
44 Home Town, Any Town
45 Water Prizes
46 Leather Windows
47 The Little Lowertown That Could
48 A Strawberry Valentine
53 Season Strokes
54 Off To School

55 Gracy Zaps NYC
56 A Lovely Walk, It Is
57 Zelium Week
64 Success Rules for USA Artists
66 A Runaway Artist Writes Home
68 Moonbreak
69 New Balances
70 You Can't Push a River
71 Ode to Kensington Gardens
72 Waiting for the Past
74 Beating Hearts
75 Scared Smoke
76 Fades of Night
77 Daft Age
78 Packing Light
79 Passengers
80 Breaktime
81 Lily Pad V.
82 Harbor Blizzard No. 1
83 The Long Arm of An Oven
85 Pearl

ANCESTORS ON HILLSIDES

Ryan, O'Brien, McCarthy
Sullivan, Kelly and McGonigal,
Crosby and O'Halloran,
then up the cemetery road a bit
Leahy and Gallagher.

We are swept
by a ritual flood,
like a stick, tossed along,
pulled to ancestral currents,
snagged near family markers
and forced to grab for life-rings,
our hopes for our own future,
and in this stream
bedded with empty shells, our breathing
seems not to license us at all
as bosses here.

We accept our ancestors
lying below us,
in this theatre, as cast
never conceding our own roles,
protesting, of course,
well, we are still in rehearsal, thank you.

Nora, age four
Michael, killed in war

Nell, in childbirth
Daniel by a thief
Kathleen.
James my father
Grandfather Michael,
the Senator Cornelius
Vic and Bart, priests
Aunts, all five, Crosbys,
Grandmother Sarah, I never saw.

Memories float
as inside videos
we offer flowers,
but retain our fear, doubts
knowing the great clock
will again repaint
these daisies.

And with darting glances,
we, from time to time
check a rusty cemetery gate
on the road back
as if to see, perhaps
on a shelf just outside its rusting frame
our resting dreams...
anxious we are to return
beyond this whirlpool,
this glutton of time place
like a boxer forced to his corner
in the final round.

2

Ancestors on hillsides
Kelly, McGonigle, Crosby and O'Halloran
and down each winding lane a bit:
Leahy and Heffernan

Drawing by Marilyn Taus

3

BIRCH LAKE

Morning sun climbs
Over our sleeping beings
Cheered by goldfinches and loons
Woven in pines and birches
Except for flashes of color and sound.

Sipping morning coffee, we launch
Dreams of catching a breakfast fish someday,
Dreams of elders who also gazed
Across Birch Lake's lap,

They, wondering as we do
Why today's hooks and visions
Snag and fade so quickly,

Yet forever,
Pine reed songs will ripple
In chorus surrounding our cabin,
Forever,
Her waves will kiss these stony shores.

KITCHIGUMI

(Lake Superior)

On the 4th of July you were summer blue,
we added red and white;
you contributed winds.
To our celebrating rockets
shot over your lap,
you blasted us with white caps,
fanning our laughing bodies
with wet kisses.

ANOTHER ONE FOR THE ROAD PLEASE

The horrible quietness of life:
western letters arrive too late
as do summer communications from Europe
even my telephones take long weekends
and talk too much about the wrong things.

Our growth rate and inflation
wear no watches
but my telephones do:
they've told me of fortunes,
announced my sickness, my health,
and reported to me, my trip to Spain
it would cost less.

They also gave me yesterday's weather
it would be fair,
you miserable instruments!
Winds just under 10 knots
northwest, I think you said,
now I nurse bruises
from a boom going 40
in a southeastern wind,
more real than you.

Lately, you've been asking
for a ride in my car,

I'd be better with any other hitcher,
why the highway too?
I'm sorry, I can't.

Yet, that horrible quietness of life
whispers to me:
"Just a short ride, only once,"
but I'd just as soon
grab your little antenna
and bend it.

AMERICAN MENU

There was never anyone like you
like you were all
I dreamed of you,
oh, to just touch you
it didn't matter, anywhere would do.

So I went to you
and you welcomed me in your arms
oh god, you were great,
when I first came to you
you were all,
you really were.

And all is what I dreamed of,
all is what I read about
with you, all was expected
and all you delivered...AMERICA,
but frankly, all is not enough.

MANUAL FOR LOVERS

Drain and flush old greases and residuals,
only then start your engines.

Next synchronize your RPMs,
or you will just go in circles.

Re-starts are a great waste
of energy and fuel,
shut it down for a while,
time and air clears the systems.

At the end of the Day,
with electricals off
just put your machines nicely away,
avoid blowing them up.

HOT WATER

(for Amos Owens, the Pipe Carrier)

Rolling to sea, to Red Wing,
water and life currents
rolling
river
to lower sea level points, she
Great Spirit's daughter
wears our castoffs, she
the Mississippi.

Dam, Dam, Dam, Dam,
river is fearful at this beltline
where a closing door lives
in Prairie Island's nuclear frypan
near river's land friends, who
survive on shrunk farms, who
cannot help river, they
her Indian people; her drummers
molding water rhythms to heartbeats.

Drumbeats for animal and sky creatures
beating during many lifetimes, times ours
long before the White West hit,
earth chords
singing rhythms,
songs,

the BIA, the Corps,
have not heard,
will never hear
from drums
throbbing many moons and suns,
river, river, river, river.

A great war came
another great war
river's indian friends were drafted
by white draft boards
who put them
pushed them
to front infantry lines, to
fight for this homeland
protecting our resources
for we who breathe this air
drink this water
precious air and water,
they who helped fight for it all
while their rusting tools
and waiting tractors, were sold
auctioned here
while they were buried there
destroyed in other lands
in the European White West:
a west that trapped them,
a west that took their lands,
a lonely time for river.

Only a few Indian soldiers returned
to the river, to Prairie Island
to America,
finding shrunk lands,
leased
by the West to the West:
to utility companies and landgrabbers,
who never, never go to war
but river welcomed her few people
still rolling, but scared
rolling to sea, downstream
to Red Wing.

Hot, Hot, Hot, Hot,
river moves fast near Prairie Island's bend
she can only nod to her friends
those few survivors
best to keep rolling.
She sees from her banks
clearings and the reactor
she swallows, filling her stomach with
heat of our nuclear age.

River carries her fish
fish with black spots
lamed fish that flatten
turn crazy angles
then drift like autumn leaves
floating downstream from the heat

the heat from Prairie Island,
fish that would say, as we would:
I can't believe this is happening to me.

Built for the people who want it all
the hot water at Prairie Island
the hot water of the West, the East
only a few riverbends away, downstream
on river
she is rolling now
on to Red Wing
on to the sea,
she is Mississippi.

SIRENS

In his afternoon dream,
he hears the warning sirens
wailing the earth's exit

A man without a gun,
but now with pistol,
and looking for one larger.
The beast in him came back.
Wherever he looks are fear-eyes.

Escaping to a cave on his father's farm,
he defends his youth of canned cherries,
apples and plums.

Entering, the ashen door cracks,
it is guarded only by old vines.
A crumbling foundation is nearby,
left by the house that once sheltered,
the laughter of his brothers and sisters,
and hopes of his parents.

Could it be, after all these years,
the canned food in the mason jars
would still be good?
The jars, like jewels when washed,
and the process of filling so caring,
with pride more the product than food.

To be near them is enough,
far better than return on top as a beast,
where the smoky fear turns to darkness.

CORN VOWS

Out where corn grows
I see with my hand,
cupping my eyes,
just touching the forehead;
tripling my vision.
I learned this as a corn child.

Out where corn grows
three-fourths of you is sky
surrounds you as a mirror;
a mirror of drought, of rain,
and sky powers.

I slow for tractors, a few chickens,
driving by a country church
white against summer's green slopes,
corn tassels usher sky salutes
to a country wedding.

Pickups are parked outside,
I see nothing through its small open door,
only organ sounds emerge,
only the pickups seem to be there
as if the church consumed its people,
here at the bottom of our sky,
where corn grows.

EIGHTEEN AND LEAVING

She is packed and bus ticket in hand,
my list of friends in her small pocket.
She carries also years of life
and I seem only to wave,
good luck.

A little money for her
we trade smiles, feel better
for a few heartbeats, we reach out,
without touching,
knowing human circuits are hard
Machine circuits seem better,
the only ones doing well.

We are an awkward process
but my aloneness joins
ancestors around our time corner
who shared our awkward waves.

We are still not doing well,
maybe better if done by machine,
that is, except our kiss.

PHOTOLAND

they are in a one room suite
  telling lies
    telecopying
      around the world

they are worried
  about growing older/fatter
    they do this
      a day at a time

their children
  do not rent this video
    they are new

like the Netherlands
  they all fear something bigger
    an immenseness beyond age
      that visitor out there
        who may never knock
          yet might

here the land will give trouble
  not sea or air
    what has sea or air done to you
      once rooms are left
        the land is the pirate

but they are good animals
they and their progenies
they will forage/reproduce
look beautiful/mate
purr/growl
act courageous
from time to time
in their open pasture
America

CHERNOBYL: A CLEAN SWEEP

Prpyat, a Russian prairie village
brewed from Chernobyl's job vat
barreling power for her big sister cities,
Kiev,
cities that greet and suck
her rich atomic nectar,
but want nothing to do
with the actual brewery, thanks.

Remember when her reactor three went awry
spilling her drink o'er Europe
quietly depositing eternal foam
oh so quietly butchering
fish, birds,
and she vomited then
with ghost breath
upon herself
upon her very own children.

Oh Chernobyl, did your bartender
go mad at the end of that day,
before your runaway
leaving the patrons
to lock up the bottles
trusting the drunks to close?

Committee inspectors claim
she's cooler now
and they mention
our Love Canal,
our big city mega power thirsts
those urban patrons
of unseen nuclear breweries
don't bother us
we all share, they say
we are all nuclear sisters and brothers
working in Lady Macbeth haste
to wipe away
such perpetual wastes.

Good bartender KOMBINAT
we welcome your latest assurances
that Chernobyl is much better now
your hundreds of photos
showing
you've swept so very, very well.

A TRIBUTE TO A YOUNG RUSSIAN PAINTER

What color and shape is freedom,
Dostoyevsky, Mandelstam, Pushkin and Brodsky,
does it come and go as youth
born again with different parents
another time, another place?

Is it bone, shattered or gray
with the color of humanity's rust,
is it blood, spilled from our internal oceans
or sky and its blue bird gases
creating our hats, no hatter changes,
is it the dark of lake's face to cumulo nimbus
as we once again pull in our sails?

Deep from the bowels of our planet
from the color collage of our ancestors
speaking to us in one tongue
these brother and sister spirits have shown us,
we are the shape and color of freedom.

MR. CITY ON SABBATICAL

Divorced from language
they flounder,
opened cans
searching for their long eaten fruit
accepting first one ghost then another
to fill their hungry wombs –
in an illusion
meandering to spinning compasses
in their poverty of communication
they rape flowers,
then rape cheap jewelry
as their broken minds chase
the dumplings in the developer's soup,
as if we will all stand on dung.

Oh, manics where are you?
saviors of America
living in squealor fiefdoms,
quit dreaming of your mothers
your mothers
are incommunicado
your fathers are now only shadows –
take off your running shoes
and put them against your heart.

In the city
should we decide to have rats

or rat licenses,
inspectors,
the state lie,
or lie in state,
creators
or administrators,
goals and objectives
or perspectives.

Help!
I may be,
Wounded Knee
Belfast
Chernobyl
Panama City
Detroit,
but don't devour me.

Mr. City come back,
beardless Abrahams
roam
our lawless urban deserts
prying open, flasks
selling
moisture,
selling secrets and
our freedom.

Look to the sky you say,
only
weather
is
in
a
sky.

Mr. City has gone to rest and write,
a full mind in death is always better
but he leaves us a note:
    kill cliches
    no more paradoxical life
    exorcise adverbs
    rotate evil empires
    a humorous species cannot kill
    exposé is a waste
    God is a comedian
    stop the mimicry of art
    a tide does not discriminate
when this is done, then I will return.

AN AUTUMN HILLSIDE

Climbing,
looking back we study fall
those magic days of autumn
falling color,
color that carries a backpack of smells
and down, over there
the hill's valley mate,
river
almost hidden, a present
glistening through sloped forests,
a blue ribboned curve.

And for the first time in a long time
leaves land on bare runways
ignoring wind's brisk direction,
they chase each other
twisting and turning
snag, then roar loose
like a hillside of puppies.

While in the valley below
a pub crew holds out for summer
as they do every season of the year,
prairie punks pounding their power pianos
accidentally serenading the hill world
as their dancing pleasure nannies
do the jerk and jump of newly headless hens.

We listen, pause halfway up
maybe not to return
then finally we descend
slowly aiming towards the
valley noise
accepting winter's orders.

Drawing by Lee Clapsadle

CONVERSION

They exploded out our doorway,
beating the sun,
morning arms grabbed their short shadows
before they grew,
cliche arms hidden in the bushes, fancy bushes.

Nowdays short shadows is all you need,
don't be a grandpa, who needs long shadows
short is good enough.

Those bushes with the huge leaves
we thought they were down our lane
not just outside our door,
those childsnatchers
performing ghosts of truth
hidden so fancy well.

ESCAPE FROM TOMORROW

We buy our holiday tickets and wait on benches,
hardened by delay after delay, then hallucinating sleep
holds us hostage too long as one creeps by us on Track 2.
Our eyes hunt for its escaping caboose lanterns,
there they are: one red, the other green,
chasing along the curved rails, then disappearing
in the outbound fog as if eaten.

We resettle, starting our watch and I recall church pews
of my childhood turning to stone by communion time
then my bottom to stone too, by benediction.
Only our young imaginations saved us from madness then.
Are we going to miss our holiday? Mike asked,
as I return from my childhood to his father again.
He warns, we must never, never miss a holiday.

There is always another holiday, I remind him
perhaps a day reading,
or seeing freely your life,
or maybe only a day to escape from tomorrow
as the past creeps by on many tracks.

PAPER AIRPLANES

Takeoffs, Monday-morning takeoffs, we hurl our power-suits
skyward in shining metal cylinders, climbing to the rising
sun. I dream they fly through my watching window, circle,
exit with great flaming torque, then burn their ritual into
the overcast sky soon to visit USA's worlds of takeovers,
mergers, acquisitions. Their ships are cargo-laden with
reports and coffee and how they win the fight against gravity
is all quite magic.

Landings On Friday: my airport window will report sightings
gliding earthward, around six, in the setting sun, acting far
less rambunctious, except for a few yet farts now and then
to keep off our chimneys...and I wonder what they've done
with all that paper: Did they dump it over some sea
prairie, or in some corporate vat brewing a new tax
concoction...or have they lugged back more?

The President interrupted Rob and Mindy's favorite sunrise
TV program. He arrived at the White House press podium
in smiles as if posing for stamp and coin artists, who, with the
quiet power of a graphic swish could make his face an
adorable or mean one for centuries. Baby Robbie watched
his excited parents from his corner of the kitchen. He even
stopped pasting his baby food breakfast on a newly painted
wall near his highchair. The President cleared his throat and
then spoke: "The Cold War is over...for all practical
purposes we won...this gives the USA, our whole world,
and our Soviet brothers and sisters – all of us on this
planet – the green-light to relax. There will be no more
deficits for dogmas."

Mindy and Rob danced a few circles in their condo kitchen.
Although the morning sun was just beginning its daily
flight, jubilant paraders from Windendale's nearby mall
were soon heard through the kitchen's open windows as
they launched a celebration over this joyous news. Mindy
smoothed a tuft of little Robbie's golden hair as she
whispered to him that he would be the last of the Cold War
babies. "Wonderful, just wonderful," shouted a beaming
Rob as he too patted their son. The TV screen showed, for
once, a cheering Washington press corps as the history-
shaking program and commentaries ended.

Rob and Mindy began sorting for storage all their peace and
Freeze campaign items from the last fifteen years: mementos

joining the past in just one electronic wave of the President's TV wand. Rob carried his heavy marching shoes; through their dusty worn coats, their red and yellow paint splotches, seemed to celebrate with him as he placed this part of his past carefully in a thick bag – then high in the garage attic. Mindy shouted toward him as he shuffled through the back door: "Hey Rob, forget Star Wars...nuclear worries... and no more fears that little Robbie will be blown away before he grows up."

Rob smiled and nodded his head toward Mindy. He frowned a little and mentioned to her, "I was just thinking about the last part of the President's speech...I just never thought we'd slip from the Cold War into Trade Wars." Rob felt a little guilty about throwing any cold water on such a good news day. "I'll tell you though Mindy, this White House telecast beat them all this decade, that's for sure...Maybe the best since the Vietnam War ended. Surely the planet must now be saved...yes I think it is...for a while anyhow." But he scowled when he thought about the President's declaration on foreign travel and trade changes. Mindy shook her head toward her frowning husband. She suggested they go upstairs for a better view of the nearby celebration. A speaker would begin soon on the splitting up of peace dividends: the President had suggested an immediate national caucus on dividing up the billions of dollars in Cold War savings.

As Rob rested with Mindy in their newly decorated upstairs bedroom, he reminisced about the Sixties and the Freeze movement during the Eighties: he recalled donating to many groups during those Cold War years. "I've always tried to do my part," he started..."Paid taxes regularly, kept good records and voted in every primary and general election. At work I was the first to stop telling ethnic or gender jokes, and I never restarted like the others have done either. Last year we made this condominium investment after years of work. Little Robbie arrived just six months ago; our family and life plans are on target." Mindy nodded in agreement. She indicated that her travel agency in Windendale's mall was ahead of last year in sales as traveling Americans scooped up foreign goods and defense contracts in record numbers. They both agreed, this was the chapter in their lives for international travel.

Rob twisted off his shoes and stretched out in the skylight's afternoon sun. He studied the fuzzy brightness as if tracing some flashing message; one just beyond his eyesight. He told Mindy, "It's good to have these things over: the missile arguments, nuclear threats and Star War debates... and reaching an end to mountainous defense deficits. Nice to know the Freeze program and all the rest worked too." He tried, but he couldn't doze off for a nap. Instead he gazed out the bedroom window at dancing and singing students in the boulevard and muttered: "It's pretty damned unfair...the President asking all of us to buy American and help picket the international travel agencies, credit card, airline and foreign company headquarters for his...what did he call it?...'Peace Through Exports' program."

Mindy's spirits continued to dive as she watched Rob's frowning face. She knew their global travel plans were now questionable with the proposed Trade War travel audits announced by the President in the later part of his telecast. She recalled how Rob had planned their trip for years. Even the Mercedes deal in Munich, at 35% off, was ready to go and confirmed via her friend's telex a night ago. Their plans called for a flight on Lufthansa direct, with departure three days away. They planned to pick up the Mercedes over there next Wednesday, selling it back here when they returned. Rob figured this "leveraging of the trip," as he called it, would nearly pay for the trip's bills. Mindy decided

to pep things up — she hated downturns of any kind. As she
eyed the demonstrators out their window she turned to
Rob: "Hey Rob, it's got to be a piece of cake compared to
those Cold War years, lighten up, will ya."

Mindy's comments nudged Rob to consider some positive
points about the Trade War: great opportunities to export
and earn bonus tax credit awards, now that importing
would be a crime. Maybe he could even write a best seller
about this fortuitous time in history, earning royalties from
his book, a book that would be read proudly someday by
little Robbie; if Rob hurried he could be one of the first
authors of the West — such a book should sell like hotcakes.
His new thoughts about the Trade Wars enthused him. He
knew he must move quickly as other books would soon be
promoted, books revealing their authors' unique role in our
planet's final Cold War chapter.

Rob made changes in his life to launch their global travels.
"I quit playing bass with Milo's Drug Free Band last week,
did you know that Mindy? Three years I played...three years
of my life...and it was a big part of our weekends. I did it so
we could devote two months to world travel per year, but
I don't know, our trips could be threatened by this damned
new policy of the State Department, the 'Bottom Line
Travel Visa,' limiting international travel to USA exports...
what do they want me to do, go to Germany and bring along
an Oldsmobile each time?" He thought about his sacrifices.
When he glanced in the corner of their bedroom at their
packed and waiting luggage, a sheet of frustration came
over him — he felt like smoking again.

While holding his head he paced the bedroom floor. He
made short kicks now and then toward the eager-looking
suitcases. Their colorful decals had made him promises. He
read them: Amsterdam, Kuala Lumpur, Basel, Lyon.

After Mindy finished telephoning her friend Nancy, she stood by Rob. It struck him then, as he watched the students, that they were all children who knew nothing but the nuclear age as their world. No wonder they were mobbing around the mall outside, still in their tenth hour of rejoicing. They reminded him of his own role in the great demonstrations of the Sixties.

"Here's the latest report from Nancy...she says: 'We're in the Trade Wars now, and they could be worse for business... than the Cold War ever was.' Remember the President's message to us this morning about winning the Trade Wars the way we won the Cold War?" Rob could not remember the exact terms used in that part of the morning speech; years of memories during the day had scrambled it – the balance was wiped away by seeing a good thing turn to bad for him. He asked Mindy in a soft voice about foreign travel bans. Looking away from Rob, she told him: "Yes, they will come into effect at midnight tonight."

Mindy curled her arm around her gazing husband. It had been a long day, this first day of Cold War's end; she made no attempt at humor. They watched their first Trade War demonstration, observing two college students, known regulars from Mindy's group, picketing the Blue Star travel agency across the street. Other students ran down the boulevard pulling ripped-up foreign travel and Visa banners, while waving a large red, white and blue sign that read: "Be American Stay Home," while shouting "Hell no, we won't go." "Idiots, just goddamned idiots," Rob shouted.

The streets outside were still flowing with dancing and laughing students, well into that night. Rob hardly slept. Around ten, Rob thought he heard by the mall the old "We Shall Overcome" song. He thought he heard the song, but he wasn't sure what was real any longer. He never imagined the Cold War would end one day like this. Shaking his head, he jumped out of bed and started to do what every good American must now do...unpack.

A HILLY PERSPECTIVE

snow whirlwinds chase my tires down your country lane
as window lights ahead poke through speeding snowbugs
softly attacking my windshield,
those lightbeams from your country house
a hill capping child of dreams that still survives
guarded from America's urban assembly lines
only by large porches.
your disappearing fencelines, orchards and workhorses
return now only as backyards and pleasure ponies igniting our fears
of a premature birth or a funeral or some of both.

you could tell me how, during rainy periods
valley dwellers looked up while sloshing
wanting you
that your horses possessed unhorselike powers
always looking down
and how for fifty years your founders commanded your knoll
then held an auction and retirement party on the same day
keeping only your farmhouse, now
then immigrating to a big city high rise
again to a "high up" place,
number 2801, top floor with a river view
because the others worried about fires
they had heard of the "Towering Inferno"
and knew they would die in one for sure
after all those years on the land

after all those droughts and grasshoppers
after all those injuries and risks
after all that sloshing in valleys
to burn to death
on the 28th floor
this the others
refused to do.

my dearest, rents you now
still above the neighboring lights
and before you and her
there were many test flights
as most singles,
romantic ads like shopping lists
ski and jazz groups
amazing fix-ups by close friends
doing what they thought best,
but how could they have misjudged
one's essence so.
worse, the fixers expected reports
how one changed, how to explain
prefer less manic types now
maybe even a reader
like she
in your farmhouse ahead.

A roar of westbound jet engines
join sky flakes in your sky
reminding me of California,

California with her rolling tide waves
waves carrying the great Pacific's speech
greeting trespassing feet
with surprising tidal fingers
always calling one's bluff
wetting one's pants legs
with the great water that never freezes.

sky thoughts fade
as the country lane's end
delivers her open door hug.
she carries the unmistakable presence of life forces
whose blessings age would never steal.
We fix to the same daily star,
but when this starts;
at five o'clock for flowers?
at seven o'clock turning down her hilly lane?
or mid-afternoon when she always opened
as the main feature in mind?

you remind me old hill
that there is a Spring of things
a Fall and Winter
flowers between us could turn to work
and we blind to their miraculous beauty
sacrificing them to the gods of rust
then dances would close
and age shut down the end of the day,
from generation to generation

a ritual all too common, old hill.

but to you old hill
we join you in our love
that the worst sin of all:
is taking beauty for granted
we honor you in carrying only the present
and carrying it well,
to the past,
we agree with you old hill:
Mr. Past just take a number and wait
when you bully to the front of our line
and maybe you Ms. Future,
you deserve the same.

HOME TOWN, ANY TOWN

news fled across town
 of mortals
  their incredible losses
   and crawled through the hairs
    of a plentiful supply of open ears
     news once inside
      attacked the soft brains
       in one fashion or another
        once the season visited
         of being age thirty or forty

news of those unfair acts of gods
 that bring moments when we see ourselves
  clothed as another, stuck in their web
   to be eaten next by the spidery past
    if only in our minds, that's enough
     that's enough then to declare
      my ears are for music and bursting waves
       not for the sound of folks about folks
        telling haggered littanies
         about expectations delivered stillborn
          about entombed and bombed-out ideas
           or those great devil successes
            no
             I'm not sticking around for that.

WATER PRIZES

We pick Autumn flowers
river daisies, small pink roses,
waterway neighbors,
while Southern travelers, overhead
fly pulsing V formations, and
announce a high sighting of Winter.

One perky mallard, swooped us
as if to call, one last call,
a duck warning we rejected,
what did he know, heading South this soon?

Long into Winter
those daisies say October
in dry sunburst yellow,
greeting us, these prizes of Autumn,
as we escape Winter through doors.

About St. Patrick's Day, a traveler returns
up the Spring river, quacking
to ask me how it went.
I see sun-tannned feathers,
and never ask back, for I have
my prizes of Autumn, my dried winter flowers.
No dumb sky creature would understand.

He bought a city view
at least 30 stories high
bought a painting – blue
bought a sculpture – round
swiveled, swiveled, swiveled,
'   in leather circles
while practicing law
at least 480 feet off the ground.

The walnut sculpture – round,
that painting of sparkling blue,
the only ones with time
to watch such a view.

THE LITTLE LOWERTOWN THAT COULD

Here is the Parthenon,
North, through the park,
Picadilly Circus
on our sidewalk
sights of Parisians,
shaking their heads
at the Germans
always too happy,
away from home.

Out of my studio window, once
my roommate even heard
people from Kansas, below,
but I didn't
there's a lot going on here in Lowertown,
you can't always catch it all.

"Why not spend Valentine's weekend visiting my mother?" Mindy asked Rob.

"Why not?" replied Rob. Years earlier, when Rob and Mindy were riding that great spiritual swirl – youth – at a place south of London, the Dorking Village Pub, Rob asked Mindy to marry him. As Rob lay the question of marriage on the pub table that night, they each recalled their rocky journeys scouring the planet's social pads in search of a mate. Then, trusting as a child does that an unstamped valentine will somehow find its destination, they came to this resolution on marriage: they agreed, "Why not?"

Grandmother, Mindy's mother, who packaged Mindy for distribution, was Mindy and Rob's mission on this Valentine Day weekend trip. The Old Woman of the North, as she was often called, still commanded the dying family fortune showcased by its headstone, a mansion: a sweeping monument on the Great Lakes' western shore.

When Rob parked their new recreational vehicle underneath the mansion's towering granite veranda, Mindy gently handed her son Robbie a big red box topped with a large scarlet ribbon. The boy wrapped his long, skinny arms around this bright cube. He studied the third floor windows as he skipped toward his grandmother's house, the place he called "The Castle."

He spotted his grandmother waving slowly from her partially opened window. He replied skyward to her wave: "Oh, Grandmother...we baked a strawberry valentine pie... Mom and I did...from berries we picked just for you last summer." Little Robbie's statement of pride was practiced with his mother, back in the city the day before.

The old woman's wave threw the estate's security switch — instantly transforming Rob, Mindy and Little Robbie from trespassers, shut out by unsmiling servants, to welcomed family.

Later, inside that great mound of brick, Grandmother's brown specked hands dealt out photos to Rob, Mindy and Little Robbie as they encircled the Old Woman of the North, while sitting on her bed shuffling faces of past days. "Yes, there you were Mindy, at seven, holding a valentine you made for me out of cellophane that year." Pointing at the faded mirror of some past day she handed Mindy's picture to her. Mindy saw the young woman — the untouched girl body — still herself: rich, very rich, but wanting instead a touch, a hug, a backrub, a trade Mindy could never pull off.

The three circulated the photos, and their faces formed a necklace around the Old Woman's bed. Outside, the great iced lake watched through hundreds of small windows, framed in walnut finished grids. The great lake, a blue paradise until recent days, looked more like a huge winter grave; it would open only in May when southern winds returned to northern shores. Inside, the four were finally alone. Mindy gave a sigh of relief as she watched the last of the servants, Minnie, the cook, disappear on the woods trail.

Through those walnut framed windows, Mindy's thoughts joined the evening shadows crawling from shore on the frozen mirror. This old mural for her drew memories of her childhood, and she was soon back: skipping along her child's shore, a shoreline where kissing lake sprays touched her wet and growing body each summer. She caught herself murmuring aloud, "Just rocks and ice, just rocks and ice now." Her child world opened here each day with the lake's sunrise. And at the end of each day, only her huge water friend, her lake, knew her secrets — he was her father — her only daily witness throughout those precious dreaming years. This great lake did not touch her now. He did then. He was the only one who touched her, never her mother. This is who Rob married.

She married this kind of fellow: after acquiring the necessary resources to sustain his planet life, Rob continued to forage for a more powerful menu. Rob spearheaded efforts to develop their area. Before importing had become a crime, he developed the largest Import-arama, featuring thousands of boutiques from the world marketplace. It was christened one June with a rosary of 37 country flags flying as a crown. In recent years, and due mainly to bitterness about the USA's role in the global economy, Rob became regional director of the Anti-Metric Movement. When asked, in a recent article in *Promotion Plus* magazine, about his accomplishments, why he did what he did, Rob replied with the same recipe that launched him and Mindy into marital orbit, "Why not?"

Before Rob, Mindy and Little Robbie left the Old Woman of the North's bedroom to fix their special supper, Rob and Mindy brought out for her their clippings, showing many cruises, their polo horses, and dinners with stars such as Sammy Davis, Jr. When the three finally left for the kitchen, the Old Woman, herself a world traveler in her day, sorted curiously through the rest of Mindy's clippings for more travel articles. Instead, toward the bottom of Mindy's clip file, her eyes fell upon one newspaper story after another describing Rob and Mindy as deeply in debt and borrowing heavily on their trust funds. Her shaking hands held clipping after clipping about what she had only heard through rumors. She had warnings. She recalled that the trust company lawyers always were negative about Mindy, but she had hated their prying. Besides, Mindy was all she had, all she ever really had after her own father's death. She felt very cold and alone. In her mansion now, very large with darkness, this Valentine's night, she thought of phoning one of the servants, or her nurse...she started to dial...then quickly hung up as Mindy came in her bedroom to wheel her down for the supper. On the way Mindy reminded her of of her favorite strawberry pie, made from summer's last strawberries.

Mindy led the Valentine supper prayers before the Old Woman of the North, who buried her face in her cupped, aged hands as she bowed over the head of the table from her wheelchair. When the prayers finished, Little Robbie, who had decorated the great mahogany slab with pink and yellow hearts, skipped around to hug his grandmother as he said, "I love you Grandma, you are my Valentine." This also was rehearsed the day before.

The glistening red of Mindy's heart-shaped strawberry pie caught the candle reflections as waves often catch sparkles from sun rays; a blazing scarlet pie decorating the middle of the magnificent wood table. As Little Robbie lighted each candle circling the special Valentine treat, the Old Woman's face shaped a smile. Across from her, and seeing her smile, Rob quietly downed his seventh scotch of the night.

The Old Woman of the North was served the only slices from Mindy's scarlet heart surprise – slices specially prepared – Valentine fruits of another kind...laced with Mindy's recipe for life. One serving would have been enough. The Old Woman quietly devoured all three.

Some hours later that Valentine night, when the bright hospital lights in the emergency room painted Rob's liquored face as red as the scarlet fruits that passed another soul from earth – and as the source of their new rescuing wealth slipped into death before them – Rob asked Mindy, "Why?" She replied with a palms-up shrug – "Why not?"

SEASON STROKES

Spring buds announce
emerging queens and princesses
dancing naked
in a new green world.
And with ease and modesty
these new April leaders
launch spring's true royalty
as they join old plant neighbors
veterans of one more winter.

Oh, those confident, sunny daisies
mixing with torched zennias
beaming, as they bow
only for summer's quick winds.

Then as summer marches through Labour Day's door
autumn will clothe these seasonal prizes
in browns and grays
spotting leaves
like time's roughdraft
on our hands and faces,
seasonal paintstrokes that splash marks
before November's cold and waiting graves.
But of course those fallen chlorophyllites
accept their winter fates
still praying a bit as we would,
they are really perennials.

OFF TO SCHOOL

Our common wall hides their murmurs,
but shouts escape from mother and daughter,
rainy school morning rituals, last instructions,
while an umbrella is chased then captured.
They are chapters 40 and 10 this rainy day,
and they speak as if this is how they'll always be
locking up time as a camera, while the newfound umbrella
just goes along for the ride, of course.

GRACY ZAPS NYC

Today my sister made it big
She wore a marvelously misty
lavender-pink shawl, ivory wool jeans.
all from B. Altmans, White Plains.

Oh, it is true, she drove away
herding an allergy free Jaguar
without a trace of liquor or smoke
fouling its leather, leather, leather,
a trained car blending art and machine.

On this delicious morning
she stopped by church
after writing our aging father,
he lives in Nebraska,
her only male illusion.

And the only palace in the world
where the Queen stands guard,
is her stay this night,
of the day my sister made it big.

A LOVELY WALK, IT IS

Me and my briefcase
blended into a briefcase stream
black, brown and gray,
scurrying to this morning's jobs.

Yesterday I was a cloud
fuzzy, drifting, unemployed
eager to form any shape
just to stay afloat.
Today I am a thunderstorm.

ZELIUM WEEK

Plinny and Marta rebelled against joining their Uncle Ollie
on a seaside trek in his Plymouth; they wanted those days
for Zelium Week. When their new parents Ruth and Jim
hesitated to agree, the two children then divulged news of
Uncle Ollie's dirty videos, a move that quickly won them
their desired week's asylum. Plinny and Marta then wrote
"Zelium classes" through the third week of their July
calendar and returned it under Plinny's bottom bunk
mattress. Zelium classes began several years ago following the
the death of J.B. Zelium. He left over one million pounds to
the student Micro Achievement Fund. Mr. Zelium had
designed and built the world-famous Zelium Towers. These
towers embodied no 90-degree angles.

In the first year only a few children attended. Later,
foundations and schools with superior Liberal Arts teachers
marketed the one-week Zelium summer program. As
entries surged, Plinny and Marta, along with other early
teenagers, vied for the coveted class berths, because the
accepted students received preemptive rights to return
year after year. Zelium's trust agreement provided: "The
money shall be used for the public purpose of teaching our
City's children to always honor nature's forces, whether on
land, in the air or at sea; these financial resources shall also
be used to launch planet sculpture courses utilizing the
Zelium non-linear method. They shall be morning classes
lasting a week each summer, culminating in a parade no
longer nor shorter than one curved block."

Plinny and Marta were adopted by Ruth and Jim Bleeker shortly after the children, then aged seven and eight, had lost their parents in a fiery small-plane crash. Little had remained after the crash for identification of the bodies. The chief crash investigator secretly gave Plinny about all that could be found from his dad, a very soot-ridden pipe lighter. Plinny recalled the nights in their family sailing sloop when his father would light their brass kerosene lantern by this lighter; he kept the lighter with that marine lantern underneath his bunk. Soon after burials, at a meeting of relatives, Ruth and Jim were chosen as best to raise and adopt Plinny and Marta. No will was found for guardian instructions. Until this tragic event, Jim and Ruth Bleeker had lived without children in the newly rennovated Paz Avenue neighborhood. They directed their lawyer to immediately sell the estate assets and sue the plane manufacturer to provide for the childrens' education. All the other relatives promised to help out as well as time went along.

Plinny and Marta were accepted for this summer's camp. During a camp planning session, they were assigned the task of securing a use license for the Zelium Camp Week. But after filing the application in the City Hall Parks Department, a license inspector revealed to them that another group had already applied for use of Zelium Park during the same week. They were told by the inspector: "You will need a hearing...a hearing will have to be held now that there are two different group applicants – unless you groups can agree. You need to contact the counter-petitioners. Let's see...they are a Mr. and Mrs. Bleeker on Paz Avenue. I think they head the new obscenity coalition called Upsurge." Plinny and Marta stood stiff and quiet; neither could speak. Plinny's suntanned face was somehow pale in color. Marta, too, showed reddened cheeks upon hearing this news about their new parents. When the inspector gave them their parents' number to call they

could no longer restrain their shock. They surprised
themselves with loud outbursts of cackling laughter,
particularly when eyeing each other. The young inspector,
a recent Tree Division transferee, became intrigued with
their uncontrolled shrieking. He closed his service window,
announcing, "This is the end of the day here."

They rendezvoused a few minutes later, via the young
inspector's suggestion, at the Government Center fountain
on the mezzanine level; there they recovered equilibrium
while perched above an escaping mob of City Hall folks
at the end of their day: unsoiled clerks, bored jurors, large
political men — lawyers with their hands welded to brief-
cases — a jerking and bobbing exodus through the
magnificantly sculptured portals of City Hall. Plinny and
Marta were greatly attracted to the inspector; he transmitted
a running score of sexual scuttlebutt about selected
passersby. By five o'clock the teenagers' eager ears opened a
door of comaraderie to the young inspector. He hustled
over this new threshold with relish. They agreed to aid each
other; he would mediate for their Zelium use permit if they
spied for him.

After a roundabout bus ride through Zelium Park, the
threesome arrived at the Bleeker residence on Paz Avenue
around suppertime. Plinny knocked — this was the rule
after sunset — while Marta and the inspector stood tickling
each other on the lower steps — both giggling when they
looked at one another. After two of Plinny's warnings, they
were forced to cover their mouths in what turned out to be
futile attempts to trap the snickering puffs and outbursts.
This was the first time that Plinny had come to the door of
his elders not as a child, but as an equal. Ruth and Jim
Bleeker seated him as they would a stranger. Marta quickly
introduced the inspector as a friend from her language class.
Her enormous falsehood to Ruth and Jim quickly sobered

her. She was also seated like a stranger around the Bleeker
dining room table.

The inspector decided it was time to get down to business.
"Mr. and Mrs. Bleeker, I only come as a peacemaker...
it seems your group and the Zelium camp must settle who
shall have rights to our park during the third week of this
July. As you know, Plinny and Marta have their hearts set
on attending this premium camp again, but as you
undoubtedly do not know, only today they have been
handed a bomb: they have discovered their own elders are
seeking the exact space during Zelium Week." Jim Bleeker
did not look surprised; he cut off the inspector. Ruth
Bleeker began to take notes.

Jim Bleeker placed his arms on the table in front of him;
the palms of his hands were facing upward as he spoke.
"Look, we have lived in this city for many years, and we
have lived by the law. We have just been elected officers
of the Upsurge; we have fought hard for a tough obscenity
law in these parts and now we finally have it...the third
week of July is our first convention; it is, my friend, a
national convention. The land next to the auditorium in the
park is needed for delegates to meander in...to see our
beautiful city from...the Zelium people can go anywhere.
Mr. Zelium was remarkable for the legacy of freedom he left
us. That is also what we represent. That is why this park is
central to our meeting." Ruth Bleeker's attention was still
on notetaking as Jim continued.

"Mr. Zelium endorsed only organized society, freedom, not
anarchy. In the Upsurge we believe the same. We must remain
free; it is not a burden to remain free; it is a privilege and
should not be delegated to third parties, such as religious
or legal organizations. We therefore must cast out
pornographers and filth peddlers. They represent only

60

cliches to truth. They are the true conformists, and more
like companies that urge folks to overeat. They are the soot
of our earth."

As is usually the case in such matters, Jim Bleeker's
impassioned meandering of what he thought to be a truth
in life only added to the verbal imbalance of our precarious-
ly hung planet. Besides the adrenalin rush he gave himself
and his mate, the benefits of his evening message were not
absorbed by the other table colleagues. As it turned out,
instead of expounding, he would have been much better off,
in terms of his own mortal health, had he either settled the
dispute or watched television.

For the inspector, this was enough: he was a spy for the
large conglomerate porno people who secretly contaminated
fundamentalist religious groups and freedom organizations
such as Upsurge. Theirs was the usual contamination, cash.
Using MBAs trained in strategic planning, porno giants were
soon able to manipulate these religious and do-gooder
organizations so as to advance their own huge investments
in sex-literature and movies. Their marketing maxim was
simple: the more anti-porn laws the better. Little
encouragement was needed in some parts of the country,
as hidden crusaders leaped to the forefront and shut down
many small entrepreneurs. Some were paid spies and
infiltrators; some did it all on their own. Soon the big guys
would have it all – this the inspector knew. He also knew it
was time to catch the bus home, where he would call his
boss in Houston and report another moonlight victory, for
which he would be paid a bonus.

Marta was at the end of her rope: her new parents, Jim and
Ruth, pinned success upon material gain. She knew they
would be leaders in the Upsurge only when Upsurge
contributed to their goal of becoming rich. Her parents,

before their untimely and fiery deaths, had known the possibility of wealth. They had developed one of this country's first portable ozone generators, to provide people with drug-free vegetables, fruits and water. She learned from her original parents that wealth or poverty often had little to do with personal merit, but this was not the rule of Jim and Ruth.

Plinny unfortunately believed he must solve this problem before the sun set: a poisonous tenet that has in a very dependable manner reduced the mortal population of our planet when there were no public wars. He would give – and he did give – Jim and Ruth his lovely marine kerosene lamp, the only memento left from the family sloop that Jim and Ruth ordered auctioned off shortly after the dreadful air accident. Proceeds raised by the sale of the ship were to be used, as Jim put it, "for the Kids' future education." Plinny's growing rage spawned a stretching resentment toward the unfairness he felt from life; his volunteer parents were becoming more the focus for this blame. What had sustained Plinny during his grief was the pride of carrying on as parents would have wanted – something he now felt he could no longer do.

Plinny was all at once compelled to give Jim and Ruth the treasured marine lantern, now his and Marta's, from the old sloop; he felt he must do this if they could not reach an agreement that evening on use of the park for Zelium Week. They did not. Plinny would give it, because other than his dad's soot-ridden lighter, the lantern was the only other remaining memento of his past and pride. Late that night, and in silence, Plinny laid it on the table before Jim, saying, "Here, this is for you." His startled new parents eagerly took the now-tarnished brass lantern and without questioning – they considered the transaction a warm gesture and breakthrough in relations with Plinny and Marta.

This gift from the sea was the only light still burning all night in Jim and Ruth's air-conditioned bedroom. By morning, only soot ruled the dark room. At Ruth and Jim's memorial, held in Zelium Park in conjunction with the opening of Zelium Week, the minister recalled to the shocked family: "How quickly we forget the forces of nature when we are not at sea."

VISUAL ARTS

First of all, be sure to impress upon your patrons and clients that you are not a craft artist, nor one who is developing any kind of artistic commodity for the marketplace. Read a lot. There is nothing worse than a visual artist who can paint well, but is dumb. It is also important to understand that the latest kitsch in painting and sculpture is minimalism. USA people who buy expensive cars and paintings expect this approach on canvas or in shapes. In the event you cannot restrain your inner artistic bombs, then go for a little splosh of color, especially a lot of red.

POETRY

The old rule was that if you made a rhyme in your stanzas you were dead for getting published in leading literary publications. This is no longer true. A rhyme is permitted now and then if it appears only as an accident. Keep in mind always the great gender market out there: there are enough editors and readers who still believe in the supremacy of one gender over the other. If the editors give you any trouble, compare what you are trying to say with specific scenes in Joyce's *Ulysses* and ask them why they think your point is different. As in successful singing: try to jam your vowels; or experiment as a loose-thinking painter might, letting your reader guess

about what word pictures you are trying to describe. This
can be quite easily accomplished, even by novices, by
drinking while you write or experimenting with a lot of
verbs to describe the same thing. Remember, you have
a license: no one expects you to be a stenographer of life.

MUSIC

When composing music, do not give a clear enough melody
to allow people to recall it or whistle it when they leave.
If you find that people are whistling your music, start
checking on the kind of audience you're drawing. When
singing, be sure to jam your vowels together so that the
audience cannot follow your song's lyrics, and never,
never allow those lyrics to be published so they can be read.

DANCE

Go directly to your nearest campus and take a political
science course. What you learn studying Machiavelli may
provide some of your most important dance-career rhythms.
Although your body is useful in your dance-life, it is best
to think of yourself as a spirit that is carrying on something
beautiful and good from one generation to the next. Have
absolutely nothing to do with recorded music or music
composed by living composers; this will put you on the
cheap and untried list. This is also true with minimalistic
stuff, but if you have real problems getting maximalistic,
then you might want to consider grants or franchising.

A RUNAWAY ARTIST WRITES HOME

Hello out there, I'm back
I nearly knocked myself off this place,
slippery was earth's surface
I found no help in gravity.

Thanks to sea gods for no great storms
and to land gods for roads back,
no storms are the best anchors,
as are roads back.

You told me being free was hard
you warned me of loose gravity in places,
it was you who told me stories
of those who slipped and skidded
But I spoke a fresh language

that's really all I wanted,
not the same stale paper,
or the "How are you?"
and I saying "O.K."

You see there was this painting
greeting me with the sunrise each day,
the official painting of the day,
its brushstrokes set our magnets,
then later our compasses
finally coining our phrases and our monies.

There were these hard to read
impossible to understand signs
stuck over our landscape
you had one in your yard
they read:
Do not touch me
Do not change me
Do not repaint me
Do not question me.

Don't ask me where I was
for I was where you needed me
I spoke a fresh language
in a few complete sentences now and then
maybe even a poem or two
you told me being free was hard,
but what else is an artist to do?

MOONBREAK

Oh, the things that happen
on this side of you, Moon.

In this phase of the moon
passions greater than the presidency
struck one of us.

May was the driest in history.
Yevtushenko read here Friday,
a few Americans are studying Russian.

And in this phase of you
we again denied we are mortals,
predictable as a thousand years of tides.

Watching, shy stars
played your light,
then slept during our workdays.

But why not come closer, Moon?
Do we have to make all the moves,
or blow ourselves off and land on you?

Then in your smug perch
you would record in ho-hum,
a happening this or that phase of the moon.

So how about a break
next time around,
next phase of the moon.

NEW BALANCES

Bam, pow, smash, sizzle
battling mineral waters
a lemon please.
You beat the bomb with spring water
try the stuff from Brazil,
ah, cum si, cum sa.

Night parlors outsugar beer with ice cream
while avant garde readership
craves a new tabloid,
in the chase for art.
As the Eighties flew, we nested
deep in woven pillows of rhythm
popping up from our trampoline center to peek
always taking turns
while the Eighties sailed.

We joined for fitness
ran the Rhine or so it seems
knew babies only as Christmas photos
in our softly suspended world.
They said we were so good for each other
strange how we fizzled
you had your job and I mine,
your life, my life
Still seems to be that way when you say
Oh, o.k. see you later.

YOU CAN'T PUSH A RIVER

On our Mississippi one day
came the President of USA,
by Lake Pepin, floating downstream,
running on-deck of the Delta Queen.
The only man I ever saw
running down a river,
pacing, jogging, jerking,
I doubt Navy taught Jimmy:
you can't push a river
and hear her song.

ODE TO KENSINGTON GARDENS

Warm hands outstretched
in Winter or Summer.
Bless her.

Reuniting young and old
who visit and coo
upon her lap;
my parkbench.

WAITING FOR THE PAST

what is the greatest greed
he asks in a voice
that should come from a grave
but we are alive
in Munichland, Marienplatz
waiting for the train to Dachau
all around
we with sins
worry he is looking our way
hoping
he will not accuse us
of unpaid dues
and we tell ourselves
these crazies
are all over now
especially in tunnels

what is the greatest greed
of the living
he bellows
accusing in a tone
that reminds us of rules
in a voice of pulpits
and a pitch that assumes the right to say
like certain of my relatives

or sometimes me to myself
at the end of a fretty day
and we wish our train
to Dachau would come on track 8
take us out of here
even if
to a dead concentration camp
'twould be better

then he shouts
as if throwing stones our way
eating
the past
is a wretched dinner for the living
breathing
the past
is no breath at all
for the past
is the greatest
greed of the living

BEATING HEARTS

You told me
I want to be with my own
just for a while.
I understand
hey I've been there too.
go ahead, after all
heartbreaks are like dog bites
who needs them.

We've spotted each other
now and then
she's with someone like me,
not her own kind of someone,
after all, heartbreaks are like dog bites,
you can foam up and die
or just bleed.

SCARED SMOKE

Only fallen leaves ride river now,
we watch her, but from her banks,
smoketrails creep flat and low
across the river, blown by the Northwester,
like cats in a strange house.
Prisoners we are,
now we too stiffly creep
as cats of the North.

FADES OF NIGHT

The day after, I brought you flowers
but couldn't find you, then later
you called to say, not today,
no greens, yellows and reds
or blues, with pink and orange tinges,
colors celebrating the day after;
the day after, when the late morning sun
struck two shoppers
one buying guilt, the other tulips.

DAFT AGE

Waiting for the doctor
you squint, frown
tap your canes
at my pink hair
tap, tap, tap
down bad news hall.

When I return
none of you will be here
for your springs
have sprung.

You'd better watch out
for the formaldehyde man.
You should have jumped for joy
seeing my young hair colored pink or blue,
or hair colored any color
or any hair at all.
Tap, tap, tap,
you can never have what I have
I have it all.

PACKING LIGHT

You find yourself in a strange country
without the language, but you know
you want nothing of their speeches, their rhythms
you are wise enough now to call it pain not experience
when you are screwed by foreigners;

your passport
birth certificate
your paper you
how did you get here
why are you here

without your damned baggage

you could have slipped through

you wouldn't have needed anyone:

lawyers
judges
witnesses
records

your baggage is your bed in this courtroom

there are no covers; but without it

you would have never traveled.

PASSENGERS

We rode like stray cats
aboard our patticake buses
dazed, bumping along
hostages on bittersweet routes
half fare.

Later, with longer legs
we roared through the world's paths
piloting in grown-up weather
full fare,
through foreign gates
as in-laws, outlaws or by-laws.

Dazed, we immigrate back
to the country of our youth
bumping along again
following those bittersweet routes
at half fare.

BREAKTIME

We see the games on TV
costumed for my son's day,
teenagers twirl and flash
at the end of a long Winter
tournament time.

He wants to join the throngs
downtown and lost from me
just for a while he assures
but to my words of caution,
he hears only the beating
drums of youth, down the hill.

The next day he smiles
yet explains nothing
I look at the crowds on TV,
knowing they will never tell.

LILY PAD V.

He waited for her
crouched, he watched
scanned, for her
she didn't appear.

He waited
waited for her on his new,
on his new lily pad
to show her
the latest in pads.

It was green
greener than green ink,
softer, softer than moss
softer than cottonwood fluffs,
thicker, 10 lily pads thick
insulated and cool, but
she never came.

HARBOR BLIZZARD NO. 1

Darting our way, snow-bugs escape
sky nests, forming clusters
like shots from a cotton cannon, then
bite, wet against our faces, fall and
glide — joining swells of ground-drifts.

Boat people, circle, breathing the 1st snow,
wondering together what we are facing,
trying to remember the Almanac...What did it say?
and quietly accept a Winter River...
a white Mississippi.

THE LONG ARM OF AN OVEN

Grandmother trained menfolk
trained them through their stomachs
like you train any animal.
Those sexual beasts
two appetites
later, work on the mind
don't start there.

I baked Stan, cranberry muffins,
in our little house near University tracks.
Oh, he loved them; we married...divorced
many muffins later; a marvel it lasted so long.
Well I'm back baking now and then.

Grandmother trained men, right or wrong,
it doesn't matter, for her it worked.
Myself, I see no sex differences,
we're 90% the same these days —
wouldn't work training through the stomach,
wouldn't work with my men; a waste of time.

Each December, I wrap a package
cranberry muffins,
fresh from my oven
addressed to Stan's latest address
and air express them

he's moved six times...gone through five women
since he left me years ago...now lives alone.

Shipping muffin memories
about our first batches near University tracks,
where we melted each other with youth.
Last year he said they were still
a little warm.

PEARL

We've charted our sail
reefed or full,
beyond old horizons.

From searching in cold winds
seasons before,
I kiss the morning sun
of our sweet voyage.

You are a necklace
all the pearls together
that I had only known
scattered.

Don Heffernan's poetry welds humanism to hard-earned perspectives. He paints word pictures with an Irish brush, portraying people on hillsides: struggling, usually learning, often laughing, and mostly winning.

Launched into life from a Nebraska USA farm, his hillside people rise and fall with America's prairies, waters and seas. One of his favorite hillsides, though, is Dun Laoghaire, Ireland, where not long ago his grandparents boarded a ship for the USA.